There's No
COLOR
Like MY
COLOR

WRITTEN by
Alicia ARzaga

AuthorHouse™
1663 Liberty Drive
Bloomington, IN 47403
www.authorhouse.com
Phone: 1 (800) 839-8640

Published by AuthorHouse 03/19/2018

ISBN: 978-1-5462-3246-9 (sc)
ISBN: 978-1-7283-0373-4 (hc)
ISBN: 978-1-5462-3245-2 (e)

Library of Congress Control Number: 2018903041

Print information available on the last page.

This book is printed on acid-free paper.

Because of the dynamic nature of the Internet, any web addresses or links contained in this book may have changed
since publication and may no longer be valid. The views expressed in this work are solely those of the author and do
not necessarily reflect the views of the publisher, and the publisher hereby disclaims any responsibility for them.

authorHOUSE®

Dedication

In loving memory of Gordon Klein
"Never turn your back on who you wish to be.
Remember who you are and never change
yourself to make others happy."

One cold morning in a magical supermarket Chloe the Cucumber, Bob the Broccoli and Betsy the Green Bean begin to talk about how they are tired of being green.

"Why are we green?" asks Chloe.

Bob replies, "Because we are grown that way. We didn't choose what color we wanted our skin to be. But as we age, we become more comfortable in our own skin."

When they look out on the floor, they see Tammy the Bright Red Tomato, Oliver the Orange, and Leo the Sour Lemon. They start to wonder how it would feel to be a bright fun color like their neighbors.

So they jump off their shelves and roll over to the Wizard Watermelon Wally.

"Morning Wally, we were wondering if you could help us," asks Betsy. Wally wonders what they could want.

"Can you make us into cheerful colors like Tammy, Oliver, and Leo? We don't like being green," says Bob. "We want to look more appealing to the eye so we can venture out into the world."

Wally understands why they want to be different, but before he changes them, he tells them a secret: "You see, it may seem like it's better to be a bright color but sometimes it is not all that peachy. Tammy, Leo and Oliver get judged for how they look."

"But they are perfect," states Chloe.

Wally begins to explain how fruits get bruised and are picked based on their skin color. The vegetables look at each other and say, "We never knew that. I guess you can't judge a fruit by its color."

Wally turns to the veggies and says, "I am going to grant each of you a wish to live a day as a fruit of your choice to see if you feel comfortable in your new skin."

"Really!" exclaims Chloe, "That would be a dream come true. I can finally be red."

"I can be yellow like Leo," shouts Bob.

"I can be orange like Oliver," states Betsy.

With the snap of his seeds, Wally turns the three vegetables into the fruits they wish to be.

"WE LOOK AWESOME!" shout the veggies.

Bob, Betsy, and Chloe love how they look. They hope a shopper picks them so they can see what the outside world looks like as a fruit.

No one gets chosen the first day, but they don't lose hope.

But finally the day comes and Chloe the Red Tomato gets picked.

"Look at how red this tomato is," says the shopper.

Another day goes by, but neither Bob nor Betsy have been picked. They start feeling softer as the days go on.

"I'VE BEEN CHOSEN!" shouts Betsy. "Maybe being different is better."

Chloe the Tomato is finally home and is placed on the kitchen counter. She begins to doubt herself when she sees another tomato next to her.

"How long have you been here?" asks Chloe.

"Three days now and I'm starting to turn mushy."

Chloe does not like the sound of that. She begins to wonder if changing into something different was a mistake. Betsy, the Bright Orange, is placed on the table at her shoppers' house. A young boy begins to roll her around and bruises her skin.

"OUCH!" squeals Betsy.

"I wish I were my old self again. Life as a green bean was not so bad."

Now all alone, Bob begins to question his decision in changing who he originally was. But at last a young boy picks up Bob and calls his father over to the fruit stand.

"Daddy, this lemon looks perfect for my lemonade stand," says the boy.

"Sure does," the dad says.

Preparing for his lemonade sale, the young boy asks his dad to help him squeeze the lemon to make lemonade.

"Can you help me squeeze the lemons for my lemonade stand?", asks the boy.

"Of course son," says the dad.

Bob gulps his pulp.

"Wally, I do not want to be a lemon anymore. Please change me back to what I used to be, a beautiful green broccoli."

Wally overhears all the vegetables crying to be turned back to what they used to be. So he shivers his seeds and POOF!

The vegetables are back to their true selves.

"WOW!" what an experience that was. I learned that being a green vegetable isn't as bad as I thought," says Chloe.

"I never want to know what being squeezed feels like," shouts Bob.

Now back on their shelves Chloe, Bob and Betsy feel like themselves again.

"I'm glad you finally realized that you are all beautiful the way you are grown," says Wally.

"I like being green," says Chloe.

"Me too," says Betsy.

"We are all perfect the way we are," replies Bob.

Suddenly, Tammy the Bright Red Tomato, Leo the Sour Lemon and Oliver the Orange start talking about how they want to be different colors.

"Red is too bright," says Tammy.

"Yellow makes me stand out," states Leo.

"Orange makes me look round," cries Oliver.

Wally the watermelon overhears the fruits complaining about their colors, but before they can ask him anything he shouts out, "Don't ever change who you are because you are all one in a melon!"

THE END

Printed in the United States
By Bookmasters